1

THE SECRETS
TO KILLER COPYWRITING:

How to write sizzling sales copy
that will dominate your competion
and explode your sales

BILL PRICE

Printed in the United States of America
First Printing, 2016

Idea Seed Labs, Inc
4635 S Norfolk Way
Aurora, CO 80015

Introduction

Copywriting is one of the foundational skills that any successful salesperson must employ to remain competitive in the market. It entails some basic elements that should come as no surprise: a mastery of the basic rules of grammar, vocabulary and a strong aptitude for making persuasive arguments.

There are more refined skills that differentiate capable copyrighters from the truly great ones. These include a knowledge of the psychology of the demographic toward which the copy is directed, a solid knowledge of what the product offers that demographic and the ability to put that knowledge into words. These skills take time, and practice, to develop to an effective level.

Truly accomplished copywriters can greatly increase the success of their marketing efforts. They copy they generate is always effective, doesn't require a commission when it makes a sale and is one of the most cost-effective ways to increase market penetration for any product or service. The skills required, moreover, require no money to develop and it takes nothing more than a word processor to create even the most complex and persuasive sales copy. Contrast that with the software expenses required to build web pages and engage in other forms of marketing and it's readily apparent why this skill should be part of the basic toolbox used by anyone involved in sales or marketing.

Online, effective copy also contains elements of SEO which increases its visibility to those individuals who are searching for the product being advertised. Intelligent copy that is well-written and reads easily is far more interesting when it comes up in search results than the stilted, grammatically incorrect varieties that tend to be so ubiquitous on the Internet. While the poor copy that so many individuals generate may be bad news for those who attempt to make sales based upon it, it is good news for those who take the time to develop the skills necessary for generating truly excellent sales copy.

The following book will guide the reader through the fundamentals of generating effective advertising copy. A salesperson who takes the time to develop these skills can not only generate a great amount of sales through the effective use of their words, they can also save a great deal of money by avoiding the necessity of hiring a professional copywriter or copywriting service to handle their business on a contract basis. These service can sometime be very expensive and may not produce exactly what the salesperson wants or the most effective possible copy for the product. Additionally, the copywriting process helps to create an effective sales pitch that can be the basis for many other types of marketing.

All that's needed to get started is literally a pen and a paper. In fact, this may be the best way to practice this necessary marketing skill. While a typewriter or word processor may seem like a more convenient idea, the more intimate relationship provided by pen and paper is oftentimes more copacetic toward developing this skill than those methods.

Chapter 1

Copywriting Basics: Why Not Hire This Service Out?

Those who have a lack of confidence in their ability to write effective sales copy may consider hiring these services out to professionals. While professionals can create incredible results, their services do not come cheap. In general, one gets what one pays for. Therefore, the most successful salespeople generally learn to do this task themselves. While it may take a while to learn, it ends up saving time in the end.

Sometimes, a product needs to have its sales letter written in a very short amount of time. Using outside contractors, who are oftentimes very busy, may result in delays that can prevent the product from getting to market as quickly as possible, as well. This may cause undue losses in sales for the company.

An effective sales letter is the best employee for which a marketer could ever ask. It never calls in sick. It never asks for a raise or an increased commission. It literally works 24-hours per day. Best of all, it eliminates, in many cases, the need for the salesperson to close the deal in person. How many employees work this hard for so little reward?

There are many sub-standard copywriters that come at a significant discount. While this may be attractive to salespeople who seek to get the job done at a low price, it can end up hurting one's business a great deal more than it can help it. Remember, poorly-written sales copy tends to translate to a substandard product in the minds of those who read it. When a salesperson develops these vital skills themselves, sales copy is literally free and most skilled copywriters are able to generate it in very short order. The investment of time spent in learning the tricks of the trade never stop paying off and their value only increases as one becomes more skilled at the art.

Being an effective copywriter also adds a powerful tool to one's arsenal where competition is concerned. Most business owners know next to nothing about writing effective sales copy. There's no need to be the best or even a great copywriter. One need only be better than average to enjoy a significant advantage over many of their competitors. A working knowledge is all that's required. Expertise will come with time and practice.

Like any other skill related to marketing, the fundamental principles of closing the deal apply where sales copywriting is concerned. In reality, good copywriting is simply good sales skills represented in print form.

One learns this skill as they do any other skill. Any individual who writes 1,000 words of sales copy will be better than a person who has never put pen to paper toward the effort. One who writes 100,000 words will be markedly better than one who has only written 1,000 words. While practice always makes perfect, there are some ways to make this affair a bit more rapidly-learned.

Like an artist learning from a mentor, a copywriter can learn their skills from imitation. Take a pen and paper and copy some particularly effective sales letters. Copying written material by hand allows the writer to get into the head of the individual who originally wrote it. A word processor or typewriter does not provide as a visceral experience. Actually writing the words manually on the page allows the writer to experience those words as they came to the mind of the individual who actually wrote them. This technique is used by all manner of writers, from copywriters to novelists to journalists who wish to slow down and take the time to really digest the words written by those who are masters of the craft.

Finding effective copy also entails some useful market research. Consider applying to be on several mailing lists. Pay attention to those letters that are delivered again and again by the same company. It's likely that these letters are being resent because they have proven effective. The companies that send these letters have sophisticated records on what works and what doesn't, so it makes sense to allow one's self to benefit from their experience. If it wasn't working, it wouldn't be delivered over and over again.

Place these recurring letters in a swipe file and study them over and over again. Pay attention to the wording and the structure while writing them. Notice how the persuasive argument is formed, how it is expanded upon and how the deal is closed. Don't hesitate to copy a particularly effective letter more than once. It helps one to memorize the phrases and word usage techniques that really make the letter a winner among others of its kind.

If this file should grow to a huge size, consider it more valuable for having done so. The body of research it represents provides insight into the success of other and can translate toward greater success for one's own business affairs.

Speaking To Your Audience As If You Were There

Most salespeople have mastered the art of verbal persuasion. Unfortunately, most people, whether or not they happen to be employed in sales, suffer something of a disconnect between the ease and fluidity with which they speak and how they represent their thoughts on the written page. To address this disconnect, one should analyze their in-person presentations which have proven effective and attempt to represent them as effectively in print as they would in a live, face-to-face scenario.

It's a general rule that what works in a one on one meeting will work equally well in print. Consider the way in which most salespeople speak. They make statements about the product that serve to pique a customer's interest and the elaborate on those statements by way of short, easy-to understand points that flow naturally from their original statement. In print, this can be represented via bullet points. Bullet points require very little time for the customer to read and understand and require little actual writing skill to create.

The process, of course, starts with the headline.

Writing Effective Headlines

The headline is the initial pitch and, therefore, the first impression a reader will have regarding the product described. Coming up with the right headline may take some time but the investment of time and effort is well worth it.

Before one even sets pen to paper, it's important to study other headlines. Research the market, get to know the target demographic and get into their heads. The headline should hit the reader with words that are powerful and enticing.

There are definitely some tried-and-true favorites where sales letter headlines are concerned. They include attention-grabbing words and phrases such as:

☐ Discover

☐ The Amazing Secrets of…

☐ Announcing

☐ Introducing

☐ Expose

☐ Unlock

☐ Unleash

☐ Secrets

These words are all attention-grabbing in that they imply that something unknown and powerful about to be described. These words are frequently seen in sales letter headlines simply because they work.

The headline should address some key elements that have proven effective in garnering interest for the most successful marketers.

There are four principle elements that one should endeavor to achieve:

☐ Self-interest

☐ News

☐ Curiosity

☐ Quick and Easy

The first item, self-interest, addresses what the customer wants. Any customer wants to know why they should spend their hard-earned money on the product being offered. This question can be reduced to "What's in it for me?" As an example, a headline that addresses the self-interest element might be along the lines of "How to Self-Publish Your Own Book and Make it a Best-Seller." Obviously, this heading implies that there is something in it for the reader and answers the question effectively and directly.

The news item means that the product's sales pitch should imply a sense of something new being announced. The product needs to be described as something that wasn't available before. A news headline would imply that what's being advertised is a solution to a long-standing problem that has only been addressed with the advent of the product being pitched. For example: "Finally, an amazingly simple weight loss method that always works. Lose two or three pounds quickly, look sexier and happier than either with American's best weight loss secret, without diet, hard exercise or pills."

This headline communicates to the reader that what's being offered is both novel and noteworthy for being much different than what's been available in the past as far as weight loss programs go.

Notice that the weight loss product headline is very long. A headline need not be only a few words long. Sales copywriting, where headlines are concerned, is not bound by the same rules that govern headlines written for newspapers. If a longer headline seems to constitute a better pitch, there's no reason to make it shorter arbitrarily.

A sales headline can even be two or three paragraphs long. Again, if the headline works better and sounds more enticing in a longer format, it's better to be effective than to be brief.

A curiosity headline oftentimes invokes the idea of a secret that holds the promise of generating something the reader wants. A good example of such a heading would be:

"The only way left for the little guy to get rich. Here is the uncensored message that my wife asked me not to disclose."

This headline entices the reader by leaving a lot of open questions. How does the little guy get rich? What does the writer intend to convey against the objections of his wife? This sort of headline makes it almost impossible for the reader to not dedicate a bit of time toward reading the entire pitch.

The headline appeals to a reader's natural predisposition to favor those things which offer a quick and easy solution to a complex problem. Each of the above headlines implies that what's being sold will reward the reader for following through on the rest of the text by giving them something that will make their life easier and more convenient.

They also define a problem that vexes many people and which has yet to be availed of a solution that isn't overly-time consuming, painful or complex.

It's generally a good idea to write the headline before writing the copy. It provides parameters for the persuasive argument that is to follow and defines the theme of the sales letter.

Don't be afraid to write several different headlines. It might take 100 headlines before the one that really makes the pitch sparkle comes along. This task is so vital to the usefulness and success of the sales copy that one should not be hesitant to dedicate a great deal of time toward the effort. Once the right headline is written, it should jump off the page and make it essentially impossible for anyone who reads it to not develop an interest in hearing the rest of what's being said.

Writing the Copy

Great copywriting starts with the very first paragraph which, after the headline, is likely the part most responsible for gaining and retaining the reader's interest. The technique of having a strong first paragraph is essential to any form of writing, news, fiction, political speech and the rest of it. This technique is equally important to sales writing.

The idea is to pique your reader's interest and to draw them in to the rest of the text much as it was the goal with the headline but with the added advantage of having more space in which to accomplish this task. There are certain techniques that make the logistics of this effort easy to understand. A few are listed below.

If/Then Statements

The if/then statement is a powerful persuasion techniques and one of the foundational elements of successful copywriting. Examples of this would include:

☐ "If you're trying to make your lawn beautiful, then this is the most important message you will ever read."

☐ "If you're been struggling to lose weight but nothing has worked, read on!"

☐ "If you're interested in starting your own business but don't know where to begin, what follows will let you in on the secrets of the pros."

Notice how each of these statements address the same concerns that determine whether or not a headline is good. They define a problem and a solution, they pique the reader's curiosity, they address the self-interest element common to everyone and they make the whole of affair of satisfying these many needs seem very quick and easy: just read below. Leads such as these are powerful at a visceral level and make it virtually impossible for the reader to look away once they've gotten this far.

The opening sentence also presents an opportunity for the writer to take the rest of the paragraph in a direction that will allow them to convince the reader through more evidence and the skillful presentation of what the product has to offer. The opening sentence sets the tone for what's to follow and should always set up a scenario that lends the opener to being easily followed-up with strong and persuasive that make the rest of the pitch something that naturally follows and which doesn't sound forced. Remember, a good sales letter should read in a way that never seems pasted together or scattershot.

Asking a Question

Asking customers a question is a technique common to all successful sales. It isn't, however, quite as straightforward as one might believe. In this case, the copywriter walks sort of a tightrope. The question must be phrased in such a way that the answer is advantageous toward making the sale. The question must also be necessarily restrictive, so that the reader's attention is directed where the writer intends.

Don't ask broad yes or no questions. Yes or no questions have the quality of making it very easy to inadvertently stop the sale by simply allowing the reader to make their determination regarding what's being sold very quickly and, thus, raising the possibility that they'll lose interest as soon as they answer the question.

For example, don't ask a question such as "Do you make mistakes in English?" There is the distinct possibility that the reader may make hardly any mistakes when writing and thus their answer would be "no". Of course, this also means that they would likely have little interest in whatever product is being offered from that point on as the yes or no question has afforded them a means to determine that the product offers nothing they need.

Phrase questions in a narrower way. "Do you make these mistakes in English?" would be preferable to simply "Do you make mistakes in English?" The narrower question makes it possible to keep the reader engaged a bit longer, at least long enough to offer a list of some common English mistakes and to possibly invoke one or two with which the reader does, indeed, have a bit of difficulty.

Keep the conversation open. An opening question is intended to pique the reader's interest and to make what's written seem relevant to them. Open-ended questions make certain that they can't simply read the one interrogative, decide that it doesn't apply and abandon reading the rest of the sales letter.

Shock Value

Opening with a "shocker" is a time-tested and valuable technique. This technique can be found in any sort of persuasion writing including sales copywriting. The idea is to hit the audience with something they cannot ignore for cause of the statement being made being so in-your-face and bold. Copywriters liken the effect to being punched in the face, to use a somewhat crude analogy.

Some examples of shocker statements include:

☐ "Writing sucks!"

☐ "Your lawn looks awful."

☐ "You're not making enough money."

Not all shocker statements need be so coarse as those above. Sometimes, they can shock the audience but be a bit subtler and involving. Examples of this technique include statements such as:

☐ "I could not believe this…"

☐ "I have to get this off of my chest…"

The latter shocker statements are less of a punch in the face, so to speak, and more of a shove in the right direction. The audience is being shocked, to some degree, but rather being more enticed than they are in the first set of statements. While these statements are certainly bolder than they are subtle, they also have a quality of restraint compared to the former list.

Either technique is very useful. The product and the headline, to a large degree, can be used to determine which type of shocker statement should be used.

Keep in mind that familiarity lessens impact. One may well be able to get good results using these statements sparingly and with an effort made toward placing them strategically within the copy, but overusing them will have the effect of making them lose their power and can oftentimes have the effect of making them seem trite and somewhat silly. Use this as an opening salvo, but realize that an entire page of shocker statements is likely to come off as bland and unconvincing.

Benefits vs. Features

The first paragraph is generally a place where the writer tells their story. This means answering the question and then explaining how they discovered the solution. For example, if one were marketing a weight loss product, they might open with the shocker, ask the question and then proceed to tell the story about how they discovered the weight loss program being described.

Benefits and features are two separate things entirely. To understand the difference, it's useful to understand how these items are listed within effective sales copy.

Benefits answer the questions posed to the reader. Most importantly, they answer the "What's in it for you?" element of the sales pitch. Bullet points are a good way to address the need to answer such questions. For example:

How will the weight loss program make my life better?

☐ No working out

☐ No gym fees

☐ No pills

☐ No restrictive diets

This rhythm of asking the question and answering by way of listing benefits is very effective and gives the reader the sense that their needs can be met by purchasing the product. Notice that all of these statements are concise and that they don't beg a question. This is what defines them as features. To determine whether or not a statement describes a benefit or a feature, one may use a very simple criterion.

A feature is something that invites the reader to ask "so what?" For example, "Our gym is open 24 hours per day," is a feature. So what if the gym is open 24 hours per day? What does that mean to the reader? It may or may not be interesting to them and presents to them the opportunity to simply say it's not useful to them and they'd be better off spending their money somewhere else.

A benefit, however, takes the feature and gives it a context.

"Our gym is open 24 hours per day so that our clients can work out anytime they want!"

The statement is now a benefit as it has a clearly defined end to the question. If the reader can read and statement as say "So what?", it's a feature. If they cannot ask that question after having read the statement, then it is a feature. This simple formula can help the writer use benefits and features to their most persuasive effect and prevent them from asking questions that may result in the customer simply dismissing the feature being offered as something that doesn't address their needs.

Testimonials

Testimonials are so heavily-used in sales copy that they merit their own section. As much as they're used, they're often used to poor effect and even abused. Testimonials are a resource, not a filler material to make up for poor copywriting. They can be incredibly effective provided a few simple rules are followed.

Testimonials should never open a sales letter. They should follow the second paragraph, at the earliest. They are a tool for helping to relate the narrative relevant to the product but that narrative must be told first.

Testimonials should follow the listing of the benefits. The testimonials cement the sales letter by offering evidence that the reader can trust the writer. The writer has already gained the reader's interest, listed the benefits to their products and the testimonials give the reader an expectation of what sort of results they can expect from doing business with the writer.

Testimonials that appear at the beginning of the document have no context which makes them not at all understandable. Without the narrative provided by the copy, they stand out in the open air, defining nothing that the reader has yet been made to understand.

Testimonials describe results, success and the trustworthiness of the copywriter. One must use them as reinforcement, not as a means for stating their initial case.

Backing it Up

The reader is going to want a bit of assurance before they part with their money. This means the salesperson has to put themselves on the line so that the reader can trust them without feeling a fool for having done so. This oftentimes entails making a guarantee of one sort or another.

It's a general rule that a longer guarantee is preferable to a shorter one, for obvious reasons. A 60-day guarantee is better than a 30-day guarantee and a 90-day guarantee is preferable to either. Of course, a year-long guarantee would be better than a 90-day guarantee.

Remember that a guarantee has to have an element of specificity to be worthwhile to the customer. "Satisfaction Guaranteed!" appears on a multitude of advertisements. It means absolutely nothing. Never use this guarantee. It's impossible to guarantee that anyone will be satisfied with a product and it should be eliminated altogether from sales copy.

An Offer They Can't Refuse

Now that the reader has taken an interest in the product and they've been informed of its features and benefits, assured of its quality and heard from other customers who have had good results from using it, it's time to give them something back for their time. This means making an offer. The offer should be so powerful that they couldn't pass it up without feeling a bit silly for having done so.

One way to make such an offer is to overwhelm the customers. This usually entails offering deals that comes at savings which are legitimate but which hit the customer as being almost difficult to believe. Some examples of an overwhelming value include:

"Right now you can get $1,000 worth of bonuses for only $197!"

A part of this technique is called comparing apples to oranges. It's simple and effective and works in the following manner.

"The seminar costs $5,000 but this home study course not only includes every minute of the material reviewed at the seminar, but also includes the Question and Answers section. If you buy today, it's only $697. Plus, you'll eliminate the need to travel and to stay at a hotel, which can save substantial amounts of money. Of course, you listen to the seminar as many times as you want."

In this case, the comparison is made between the two options presented for obtaining the information from the seminar. Attending the seminar is characterized as expensive and time consuming while simply purchasing the home study kit is revealed as economical and time-saving. The fact that the home study kit can be used as often as desired is also emphasized, which defines another benefit to the consumer.

It's not an overstatement to say that one should actually endeavor to make the customer feel stupid if they don't act on the offer. The benefits, price and guarantee should define an opportunity that no rational person would pass up easily. Convenience-based pitches are particularly effective toward this end.

Why would the consumer not want to have the seminar materials on-hand when the only other option is to attend the seminar live and all the expenses that entails?

Now that all of that work has been done, the most frequently overlooked and incorrectly-executed element of the sales letter comes into play: Telling the reader how they avail themselves of the product.

How do they get it? In far too many cases, an excellent sales letter, at the end, leaves the customer completely confused as to how they actually go about getting the product they've been pitched. This is one of the most critical parts of copywriting and constitutes the element of sales writing where the greatest amount of mistakes are made.

This requires a specific and clear call to action being presented to the customer. There should be no mystery as to how they place their order and the more specific the means describe the better; for the salesperson and the customer alike.

Deliver the instructions in the same direct and clear fashion as one might expect an ER surgeon to give instructions to their staff or a military commander would direct their troops. Simple, comprehensive and clear statements.

Don't say "Call Now!" Say "Call 1-800-555-1212 and tell the operator to place your order for Product X."

Don't say "Order today!" Say "Go to www.bestproductXXX.com and complete the simple order form to get your Product X shipped to you right away!"

These statements are basically commands and have the effect of giving the customer all the information they need to complete the order in a clear, concise statement.

A call to action should be followed by the instilling a sense of urgency into the whole affair. This requires specific considerations which are detailed below.

Why should they do it now? Instilling a sense of urgency into the sale is so important that it merits its own section. Quite often, this task is accomplished by making an offer that has a definite expiration date.

An example would be "Respond within 30 days and get 10% off!" This gives the customer a reason to act sooner rather than later. It also increases the element of making the offer they can't refuse.

Another example would be making an offer based upon rewarding the first X number of clients. For example: "This offer is only available to the first 100 customers."

Time-limited offers not only add a sense of urgency, they present a reward for acting quickly. When offering these soft of pitches, it's important to keep honest in mind.

The idea is to create urgency while still conveying that what's being sold is valuable and useful to the customer. This plays into the news aspect of sales writing. A product may be available on a free trial basis because it is a new product on the market or a remarkably improved version of an already existing product. It may be offered at a discount because a large amount of stock is available but not because there isn't demand for the product.

Let the customers know that they only have a limited time to get in on the deal being offered, but make certain they have adequate time to make the decision without feeling like they're being hurried. For example, a 7-day special offer is only useful for a week and will seem as if it were contrived if it's extended for another week immediately afterwards. A 30-day special offer is manageable, allows a customer to consider the purchase and still has enough of a time limit that it requires initiative and can increase the amount of sales while it is active.

Never, Ever Lie

After all that work put into gaining a customer's confidence, it would be a shame to tear it all down by telling a lie. Now, of course, a lie might not be intentional. This doesn't matter to your customer. One lie and they will lose faith in you.

If an offer is given on a time-limited basis, any materials related to that offer must be updated in accordance with the expiration of the offer. For example, if a webpage offers an enticement to the first 100 customers, it should be revised as soon as the first 100 customers have placed their orders.

This has to do with the single greatest asset any salesperson has: credibility. If the customer cannot believe the salesperson's word, how can they have any justified faith in the product itself? There are some ways to word these offers which insulate the salesperson from putting their claims to the lie.

Free trials are a good example of how one makes these accommodations to protect their credibility. If a salesperson has an offer that cannot be kept going forever while still generating a reasonable profit, it makes sense to use qualifiers that ensure that they're not over-promising. Closed, committal statements versus more open-ended, unmanageable statements can be described as follows:

"Customers will get free resale rights to this book!" versus "The first 30 customers will get free resale rights to this book."

"Free trial version available!" versus "Limited quantities of free trial versions are available."

In both examples, the latter statements are safe and the former statements too broad and at risk of becoming lies. Should a customer call in and ask for a free trial version based upon the first statement and find out that there are no more free-trial versions available, they're likely to feel as if they've been deceived. In the second statement, they can simply be told that the free trial versions have all been distributed already. In that latter instance, they haven't been lied to and they won't feel cheated, they'll simply be made aware that they acted too late to take advantage of the offer.

The importance of honesty is absolutely vital to understand. A customer who feels that they've been cheated will likely view the salesperson as a huckster and a fraud. While the salesperson may be neither and simply a victim of their own carelessness, the reputation will likely be long-lasting and difficult to remedy. Certainly, the salesperson can expect no further business from that jilted customer.

The P.S.

Every good sales letter should contain a P.S. This creates an opportunity for the salesperson to restate their case and to offer a bit more.

The P.S. should first remind the customer of whatever pain can be relieved by ordering immediately. This reinforces the sense of urgency the beginning of the letter sought to develop regarding the product. Or, as another option, one may simply restate their guarantee to offer a bit more assurance. An outstanding testimonial can also be offered in the P.S. to reassure the customer.

A good P.S. can be defined as one that could be completely understood if one were simply to see the initial headline and go directly to the P.S. and come away knowing the gist of what's being offered, what's being guaranteed and how they go about availing themselves of the product in question. It's a short, powerful means of closing the deal.

It's also an opportunity to make the letter more personal. The salesperson should attach their name to the sales letter at this point. Adding one's name to an offer is to add a touch of personal honor to the whole affair; the equivalent of giving one's word that's what being sold is worth the money and that the value of any special offers are so good that the salesperson does not hesitate to associate themselves personally with them.

Remember that there's been a guarantee offered, as well, and adding one's word to the letter tends to reinforce the value of that aspect of the sales letter.

Walking Through an Open Door

Buying a product tends to be accompanied by a positive emotional response. The customer obviously feels as if they've done well for themselves, getting a product that offers something that will alleviate some sort of pain their feeling and replace it with the pleasure that comes with having that pain addressed. In fact, some psychologists theorize that these are the two primary psychological motivators in human beings: Increasing pleasure and decreasing pain.

Once the customer is in a buying state of mind, it makes sense to take advantage of that by offering them more. Make certain that, at the end of the copy, they're offered another opportunity. This is called upselling and is a basic sales skill.

Consider the situation if one calls into a home shopping service that operates via infomercials. As soon as the customer announces to the operator that they'd like to purchase a given product, they're made aware that there are other products that naturally go along with their intended purchase. They may also be offered an extended warranty or some other bonus for their trouble. In some cases, it's actually difficult to simply make the original purchase because of all that's being offered in this manner.

The last part of the sales letter should offer a similar service. Throw in a few bonuses for a little extra money. Offer additional products that go along with the ones being offered or make a convincing segue into another product entirely.

When a customer already has their credit card out, they're ready to buy and will be easily persuaded to spend a bit more if they're being offered something valuable. This isn't exploiting a state of mind but simply addressing the customer's desire to have their most basic needs met at the time when they are present in their mind to a great degree.

Never give up this opportunity. Once the customer has been convinced, it makes sense to ratchet up the sales a bit. Upselling is an incredibly important sales technique and is much more easily accomplished than is making a sale from scratch.

Review

The basics of a good sales letter constitute the following

☐ A powerful, attention-grabbing headline

☐ An opening paragraph that cements their interest

☐ Bullet points that describe features and benefits

☐ Testimonials that remove skepticism

☐ Guarantees that assure trust

☐ An offer they cannot refuse

☐ Specific instructions regarding how to order

☐ A closing with a sense of urgency

☐ A P.S. that maximizes response

Chapter 2

The Basics of Good Writing

There are several elements that characterize any good writing, sales copywriting or otherwise. Mastering these elements can help the salesperson reach their customers more effectively and help to create a bond of trust between writer and reader.

Speak to the Client

The more personal sales copy is, the better. This means preferentially using singular pronouns such as "I" instead of plurals such as "we" or "us". The reader should feel that what's taking place is a person-to-person conversation regarding the product. Making it seem impersonal has the effect of distancing salesperson and customer, an effect that can prove negative to sales overall.

Think as if you were in the customer's own home, telling them about the product in person. In such an instance, referring to one's self as "we" would seem something more than silly. In a sales letter, it can seem equally silly and doesn't afford the air of a larger corporation speaking, as some writers like to assume.

Write the Way One Speaks

Newspapers were once derided for writing at a "5th grade level". There is good reason they choose to do so: It ensures that all readers understand what's being said.

If one has access to both a 5-dollar word and a 10-cent word, the 10-cent word should be used. This ensures that the reader isn't caught up trying to understand overly-complex language and that they can focus on what's being said instead of being distracted by how it's being said.

This is often referred to as a "conversational tone". Quite simply, it means that the tone of the writing is what one would expect if they were sitting down over coffee with the writer and simply having something explained to them in the easiest to understand way possible. It means not using words or phrases that require a PhD to understand. It's not condescending to the reader and, in reality, shows a bit of modesty on the part of the writer which is attractive and has the feel of someone who's simply being honest.

One should seek to not overestimate the knowledge of their audience. This means not using jargon or technical language when it's inappropriate. Even the great scientific writers are characterized by their ability to put incredibly complex concepts into simple, easy to understand language. Overly-ornate and gilded prose has the effect of making the reader feel that a lack of substance is being compensated for by the writer's use of unwieldy words and phrases. The tone of a sales letter should imply that it's being written by a friend, not by one's English professor.

Go ahead and write at the 5th Grade level. In fact, it pays to ask one's self if a 12-year old would be able to understand the language being employed. The customers will feel that the writer is simply being direct and that they're not concealing anything behind hard-to-understand language. Remember, what's being attempted is to get the customer to part with their money for a product or service, something that's not likely to happen if they fell like they don't know what's even being offered.

Sell the Cure, Not The Prevention

To use a rather extreme example, consider a cancer treatment. If one received a letter that said that it provided a means to purchase a guaranteed method of preventing cancer, how much would one pay for that preventative measure. Consider that many preventative measures against cancer are completely free and that many individuals still carry on with habits that are known to cause cancer, and pay good money to indulge those habits.

Contrast this with selling a cure for cancer. If one had cancer, how much would they pay for a cure? The answer, of course, is any amount and the salesperson would have to do very little work toward persuading the person.

This carries over to any product. A product that prevents weight gain would be much harder to sell than a product that makes weight loss fast and easy. A product that educates people about how to avoid making bad investments would be more difficult to sell than one that tells people how to get out of bad investments they've already made.

Assume They're Not Interested

It's best to write from the assumption that the reader hasn't the least bit of interest in the product or in even hearing the pitch. Assume your reader is the classic old cynic, possessed of a horrible attitude and a negative view of anything they're told. The writer has the obligation of persuading this person to take an interest.

Assume that, not only is the reader not interested in the product, but that they're not at all interested in the salesperson selling it. They don't care about helping a salesperson to achieve any success and don't care about participating in any special offers. The tough crowd should be factored into any sales effort and it's imperative that the writer does not assume that the reader will start out with an enthusiastic attitude toward what's being sold. If one assumes that people are lining up around the corner to buy any product, then they're sorely mistaken. All that's on the average reader's mind is me, me, me, me and me.

Don't be Afraid to Offend

Shock value is an excellent tool for the writer. In order to capture the reader's attention, it pays to be a bit outrageous.

Remember that the average reader is distracted by myriad facets of everyday life. Family obligations, money, and the rest of the stressors individuals face on a daily basis are common and powerful distractions. The writer must be singing, dancing, shouting and screaming to grab the reader's attention.

There is no real face-to-face interaction where the written word is concerned. If one feels they're taking their writing a bit far, they're likely only beginning to take it far enough. If someone isn't offended, the marketing may well be inadequate to the task.

Consider how some of the most successful business people behave. They don't come off as warm and fuzzy or necessarily someone one would want to bring to a family dinner. They're bold, straightforward, no-nonsense individuals who aren't afraid to use a word that may offend if that word is simply the best way to get their point across. They don't care about what people think of them or social approval. Do not be afraid to offend people every now and again. It's a sign that one is on the right track.

If it makes one feel timid, consider that those people who are likely to be offended are unlikely to constitute one's target market in any regard. Sometimes it's best to get a few complaints and be more effective at reaching the people who are actually going to buy one's product rather than cater to those who don't have an interest, anyway. Remember, the most successful rock stars are frequently not the best musicians in the market but they're quite often the most shocking.

Don't Fail Big

If one is launching a new product, it's best to limit one's efforts until they're sure of the actual market for it. Do the marketing in the most cost-effective way possible so that it has a chance to pay for itself in this small regard before throwing all of one's resources behind an unknown quantity.

More importantly, don't take this to be permission to sell low-quality products. One's credibility still takes precedence over most other concerns. The idea is to limit one's risk to a sensible level so that they're not stuck with a huge bill for having marketed an unsuccessful product. Should the product prove popular, one can always go back and dedicate more resources toward the effort.

Copy Is Not King

There is a common misconception that the copy is the king. In reality, the list of potential customers is the king, the offer made is the queen and the copy is more of a princess. All three of these elements are necessary to launching any successful campaign.

Multi-Step Mailing

If a product is good and it's garnering interest, one shouldn't give up on those potential customers who haven't responded to the initial offer.

One can resend the mailings with small modifications such as "I'm puzzled that I haven't heard from you" or "I'd like to offer this product again." If the product returned profit on the first occasion, it'll likely continue to do so over the course of several more mailings. Persistence goes a long way toward success.

Consider three times to be the charm. Consider strategies such as changing around the headline a bit to reach customers who may not have been enticed by the first offer. One may consider adding more testimonials to their pitch or adding additional bonuses for those particularly hard-to-convince customers.

One may well become thoroughly sick of looking at their ad while undertaking this process. It doesn't mean that one's customers feel the same way. When the ad fails to return any profits after having been used for a while, it may be time to consider ending the campaign.

The three-times rule is particularly important toward showing respect for the people on one's list. If they don't want it by the third mailing, they may well not want it at all. Assume that they're just not interested and go ahead and back off the effort.

Test, Test, Test

Skillful marketers spend a great deal of time determining what works and what doesn't. This means changing headings, changing the price and not working off of guess work. Start by determining what the best offer may be and be willing to tweak it to accommodate the market.

Look at the ways the advertising campaign is generating traffic. If SEO is a part of the campaign and if one is using Internet advertising and joint venture partners, they can be reasonably certain that the traffic they're receiving is qualified. If they're not qualified, the offer may need to be changed.

Consider changing the offer before changing the heading. Adding a few more bonuses so that a $500 value is being offered for $67 instead of a $300 value being offered for $67 dollars may well increase conversion rates.

After that, consider tweaking the headline. Try to beat one's own headline. Changing the headline, especially online, is very easy and fast.

Psychology plays into this. People like to be given a reason for doing something. Studies have shown, and most people will realize this, that it's much easier to persuade someone to go out of their way on one's behalf if one offers a valid reason. Offer the customers an explanation of why a discount is being offered.

Consider the retail model. Most retail stores simply advertise a sale. These campaigns are notoriously ineffective. However, when there's a reason put to that sale, "overstock", "back to school", etc., customers find it far more persuasive. Some savvy retailers even go the long headline route, such as: "We purchased too much of Product X and have to get rid of it so we're offering this amazing product at a 40% discount!" This goes toward developing trust and credibility. If one happens to be offering a great deal, they should always take the initiative and define why and how that deal is able to be offered.

Sell the Sizzle, Not The Steak

In most cases, writers are encouraged to write with verbs and nouns and to eliminate unnecessary adjectives. This is not the case where sales writing is concerned. The right use of adjectives can easily double the impact of sales copy.

Consider, for instance, the following two statements.

"Give me any copy and I'll transform it into a kick-butt sales letter that will practically force your prospects to buy your products and services."

Now, contrast that copy with the following:

"Give me any dead in the water copy and I'll miraculously transform it into an absolute kick-butt sales letter that will practically force your prospects to buy from you."

The second example benefits from instantly creating an image in the reader's mind. It describes not only the letter the writer intends to produce, but the lacking characteristics of the marketing materials currently being employed by the company. This clever use of descriptors can entice a reader to create their own mental image and affords the writer the opportunity to direct that image in the way that's most beneficial to them.

Remember that customers buy out of emotion. The writer's responsibility is to invoke in the reader that emotional state which is most likely to result in the reader making the purchase. The writing should hit them with a bang and make them feel as if buying the advertised product was the only rational action they could take.

Constructive Criticism and Rewriting

The vast majority of writing is actually rewriting. Don't be afraid to have text looked over by another sales professional, friend or other individual and have it critiqued for its effectiveness.

Having such critiques made of a website can go a long way toward making sure copy is tight, engaging and that it grabs the reader's attention. In many cases, a writer will read back their copy as if they'd written what they thought they'd written instead of what they actually wrote. Having copy critiqued and rewritten by colleagues and friends is one of the basic success strategies of any skilled copywriter.

Create a Story

When one is pitching a product, it's a good idea to help the reader visualize how they will put that product to use and how it will help alleviate their pain and increase their pleasure. This technique is simple, effective and enjoyable for the reader.

For example, instead of simply advertising a gym being open 24 hours per day, one may create a narrative that explains how that will impact on a person's life.

"Those who haven't the time to work out during the day will enjoy the fact that the gym is always open and that there is always staff on hand that will help them achieve their fitness goals."

An entire scenario has been created in this way, ensuring that the reader not only realizes the value of the gym but that it has an obvious role in their life and in helping them to achieve their desired results regarding improving their lives.

Use Sub Headlines

While the headline has a place of great importance in copywriting, the sub headline offers a great value, as well.

The sub headline can be used to set off points about the product that can entice the reader to keep going on their way through the copy. It can also provide a means to make the copy flow more efficiently and read more easily.

Know the Competition

If one is lucky enough to have a product that addresses a need that isn't currently addressed by any competitors, then a direct pitch can be very effective. This need only entail outlining the specific benefits of the product and explaining how it fits into the buyer's life as outlined above.

In most cases, however, there will be competition in the market for whatever product is being offered. For instance, offering a weight-loss product means that the salesperson will have innumerable competitors who have already done their sales copywriting and who may have done a better job of it than the salesperson can do themselves. In this case, comparisons are useful to making one's product stand out.

One can study the competition, read their sales copy and challenge their competitors. This means finding those needs that competitors haven't effectively addressed and making certain that one's own product is cast in a light of addressing those concerns in a way that is fast and easy. Tell them how the product being marketed is different than the competition. Tell them how it's better and be bold in doing so. As long as the claims being made are honest and true, one can use this technique to make their product stand out. While one's product may not be the only such product on the market, it can be cast as the best product currently on the market and, thus, the most sensible choice for any consumer.

Including Media

Most web copy, and a great deal of written copy, includes pictures and other media that sets it off and makes it more attractive. Formatting the media and placing it in the most effective position on the page is important.

For example, one shouldn't break up the flow of their text with an image. A great deal of empty space surrounding a picture forces the reader to work hard, to scan the page and pick up the words where they left off. Make sure your reader can easily flow with the text and that they're not distracted by sloppy placements of pictures and other media.

Chapter 3

Making the Process Efficient

A professional editor may take an hour or more reviewing advertising copy. For about $100, in most cases, they can offer a great deal of assistance in tightening up and making more effective the means being employed to sell the product. The writer can make their copy better by simply investing a few extra minutes in review.

Analyze the copy to make sure the structure makes sense. It should flow logically from one point to the next and never leave the reader wondering how they were supposed to draw a particular conclusion.

Make certain the headlines are engaging. They should really drive the reader to continue on with reading the text and act almost as a stand-alone reason to do so. The idea is to draw the reader in with the headline, firm up their attention with the first paragraph and then expand upon the concepts presented with the rest of the document which serves to make the deal even sweeter than they originally thought. By the time the reader is done, they shouldn't be able to walk away from the deal. Having an outside set of eyes check to see if one's copy achieves this is very useful and can make good advertising copy into great advertising copy.

Using a Professional

If one decides to make use of a professional editor, expect to pay money for the service and make certain that the price is worth it. Check to see the copy the editor themselves has created and see if it meets the criteria listed in this text. If their copy doesn't grab one's attention, it's unlikely that they're actually going to be able to make any lacking copy of yours any better than it already is and, thus, that their services won't justify their prices.

There are, however, very good and successful copywriters and editors available. Some of them maintain web pages from which their services can be engaged. For the beginning copywriter, paying a little bit for their services may be well worth the knowledge thereby obtained.

Using one's JV partners or friends may help, as well, but a professional in the field may be able to offer more for the money than casual partners can offer for free. If one is launching a new campaign or is having poor sales with an ongoing campaign, hiring such individuals is generally worth it toward increasing profits and making a product as good a seller as it can be.

Some of the best editors may charge a bit more for their services. Following the advice given previously, if one has a product that has a good track record of sales but which needs a bit more fire injected into the campaign, it may be worth it to go ahead and engage these individual's services to increase the overall sales of the product.

Putting it all Together

Now that the basics, and a great deal of the more advanced concerns, have been addressed, the question remains: How does one put this all together and make themselves into a successful copywriter? The process begins and ends with practice.

Find the Best Copy

Search out those instances of truly great copy. This copy need not be from small websites or independent marketers. Take a look at how the largest companies move their products. See how their copy is written and start making a file. Fill the file with whatever comes across as interesting.

Remember to keep an eye out for those instances of copy that is recycled over and over again. This copy is likely the best-performing sales copy the company sending it has and should be analyzed to see what really makes it so much better than what else is out there.

Imitation

Study the copy, read the copy and, most importantly, rewrite the copy. Pay attention to how the words flow. Study how it conforms to the basic model described in this text. Pay Particular attention to those most important elements.

How does the headline manage to catch the reader's attention? How is it structured? How does it relate to the first paragraph and what is it about the way that headline is structured that makes it flow into the first paragraph?

Study the first paragraph in detail. How does it engage the reader? What claims does it make? Does it shock the reader into wanting to know more about the product being advertised? If so, what words or phrases does it use to achieve that reaction out of the reader?

What features are advertised and what benefits do they entail? How are features and benefits related by the writer? Do they flow naturally or does it require a stretch of the imagination to see how they relate to each other? If it's good advertising copy, then it's likely the case that they flow naturally from feature to benefit and it's easy to see how the reader is to make the connection.

What about the letter makes the reader feel like they're justified in placing their trust in the writer? If a guarantee of satisfaction is made, throw the letter away. As was stated, that is the single most meaningless guarantee that anyone can offer. In fact, it constitutes a bit of dishonesty because no one can guarantee that a customer will be satisfied with a product, even if it performs as advertised or even better than advertised. Look for concrete guarantees that make the customer know that their money is well-spend and that their business is valued by the salesperson.

How is the bonus offered? Are there packages that have more value than the initial price offered? Are there add-on products that make the purchase a more sensible one than it would be if bought individually?

Of course, at the end of the letter, the reader should know exactly what they have to do to purchase that item. There should be no guess work involved, no hunting through other materials to find the needed phone number and no confusion regarding the preferred method of payment.

There should be a P.S. section to the letter that summarizes and makes more attractive the original pitch. Remember to structure this in a way that it would make perfect sense even if one were to simply read the headline and move directly to this section of the sales letter. The P.S. comes at a point where the customer has already made the effort to read the entire sales letter and at a point where they may be very inclined to buy. Make certain to take advantage of this.

The end of the letter should contain an up sell offer. This lets the customer know that they can do even better. It also makes certain that they're reminded of this fact at the time they're ready to make the purchase. This combination of skillful, enticing writing and the customer's positive state of mind is a very powerful one and can create greatly increased sales. Make certain that a related product is offered or that a value-added product is offered so that it is very difficult for the customer to pass up.

If all these criteria are met, then one is certainly looking at a good example of sales copywriting. Now comes the imitation.

Rewrite the letter, by hand, and absorb everything about it. Get into the writer's head and see how they're able to excel at this the way they do. Pay particular attention to the following:

- ☐ How they use headlines and sub headlines

- ☐ How they structure their phrases

- ☐ The sort of vocabulary they employ

☐ How they define their audience

☐ How they appeal to that specific audience

☐ How they work their product into a narrative involving that audience

☐ How they shock that audience into paying attention

☐ How they cater to that audience's basic needs

☐ How they engage curiosity

☐ How they structure the document as a whole

Chances are, there are a lot of powerful words being used. One need not delve into English 404 textbooks to find this vocabulary. Many of the most potent words are also the most frequently-used.

Good copywriters do sometimes use words that border on obscenity to engage their customers. For example, "It's really a bummer when your car breaks down" is pretty lack luster. "Aren't you pissed off when your car breaks down for the following reason?" is much more eye-catching. It's the way people talk in real life and makes the reader feel as if they're being spoken to by a human being instead of by a corporate marketing department. Check good sales letter for such turns of phrase.

Get Over that Lack of Confidence!

Readers can sense a lack of confidence when it's represented in print. Don't be afraid to write naturally. There's no need to be the best copywriter on Earth to make a successful sales letter. Keep practicing and just do a bit better than the competition. As skilled copywriters point out, the vast majority of business owners have no idea how to write sales copy. Those that do have a distinct advantage.

It takes confidence in one's self to even learn this skill but most salespeople understand that they have to believe in themselves to sell any product. Keep confidence levels high by constant practice. Remember that, the more one writes, the better writer they become. Even a person who has only written one sales letter enjoys a substantial advantage over someone who hasn't written any.

Write Your First Letter

Every journey begins with a single step. Write your first sales letter and pass it around to friends. See if it works for them. See if they'd be inclined to learn more or even purchase the item described based on the letter.

Work the letter out to the best it can be and send it out to clients and gauge the response. If response is good, chances are that one is on the right track in their copywriting efforts. One may even find that they have a knack for this task that they may have never guessed they did.

Track It

It's vitally important that one keep track of the sales resulting from one's copywriting efforts. This ensures that substandard copy gets fixed and made more effective and that particularly good copywriting is exploited to its maximum value. This is why some letter arrive in the mailbox over and over again: the companies that sent them had the good sense to pay attention and, thereby, determined that they were working as intended.

Remember the turns of phrase and headlines that worked and develop similar headlines and copy that employs those same elements. If it worked once, it will likely work again.

It is worthwhile to keep a record of all the sales copy one has produced and to look it over now and again for reference. It's easy to forget what worked in the past, but, if one has a copy of a particularly good sales letter there's no reason one shouldn't replicate it for another product. Keep track of all phases of the copy, from the initial pitch to those pitches that come later and are directed at customers to whom the first attempt didn't appeal. Remember that three letters are enough for just about any product. If the customer doesn't express interest at this point and others have, it's likely that the product simply isn't useful to them. If no customers have expressed an interest by that point, it may be time to review the product itself and to see if it's worth keeping on with the marketing project or to simply let it go.

Chapter 4

Copywriting Recap

Because so few businesspeople have actually mastered the art of sales copywriting, any business owner who does so enjoys a distinct advantage over their competition. Doing so is not so difficult as one might assume though it does require diligence, practice and follow through.

Good sales copywriting must also flow from the assumption that no reader is interested in hearing a single word about the product. Assume negativity on the part of the audience and work from a position of someone who needs to make a case convincing enough to overcome this negativity. One need not change the entirely negative attitude of the reader, only get them into the state where buying seems to hold the promise of increasing their happiness.

Sales copywriting is essentially the same as is any other form of persuasive writing. It entails grabbing the reader's attention, involving them in the narrative and leading them comfortably and logically along to reach the writer's desired conclusions.

It does require practice, as does any other marketing skill to reach the level of effectiveness, and even perfection, that is required to ensure success. The most effective way to practice it is to engage in sort of a mentorship, learning from the best examples of sales copywriting that one can find and imitating those sources while turning them into something completely new and unique.

Like any language-based skill, copywriting requires that the author adhere to basic rules of style. The idea is to grab the reader's attention and not to let them go once that goal has been attained.

Grabbing the reader's attention starts with an effective headline. This headline does not need to be limited in length as does a newspaper headline and can very well be several sentences long. It should employ clever language and sometimes outright shock value to engage the reader.

Write as many headlines as necessary, even if the number gets to be 100 or more. The best headline may not come along for a long while but it's worth it to keep on going.

The first paragraph needs to clearly define the product and appeal to the reader's basic needs. This means making appeals to the natural inclination of any human being to increase their level of pleasure and to decrease their level of pain. It needs to provide a good reason why the reader should stick around and listen to the rest of what the writer has to say.

Understand the differences between benefits and features using the simple rule: Benefits don't result in the reader being able to say "So what?" Features are open-ended and don't immediately identify themselves as useful to the reader.

Use simple if/then statements to make the product more relevant to the reader. "If you need to lose weight fast, then you need to read about this product!";

"If you need a way to make money from home, then you need to attend this seminar!" These sort of statements limit the question and don't allow the reader to add their natural negativity to the equation.

Don't be afraid to offend! The best sales copywriters understand that offending the audience is sometimes the best way to grab their attention. Don't go overboard, of course, and be sensitive to the audience. At the same time, realize that if something is borderline offensive some very accomplished copywriters take this as a sign that they're on the right track.

Keep track of what you've written and see which sales letters are garnering the most success. These sales letters likely contain characteristics that can be used over and over again without losing their effectiveness.

Remember to rewrite ineffective sales letters and not to give up too easily. Get personal with those hesitant customers. "I haven't heard from you in a while and was wondering if you'd seen this new product," and similar statements drive the point home and make the whole affair more personal to the customer. Remember that the customer should feel as if they're being directly-addressed and that they're not simply the recipient of the latest corporate sales letter to be sent out bulk rate to thousands of clients.

Throw out your style guide. The advice that writers should avoid adjectives does not apply to sales copywriting. You're not selling a weight program, you're selling the best weight program out there and the amazing results are something that those who suffer the horrible anxiety that comes with being overweight need to be informed of. Remember the axiom "Sell the Sizzle, not the Steak".

Remember that those sales skills that apply in person apply equally in print. While writing, engage in a conversation with the client. Use the same persuasion techniques that work in real life. What's being used is language and the effects of language are largely the same whether it be of the spoken or written sort.

Have your efforts proofread and critiqued by friends and family. Better yet, hire a real editor. Don't take any harsh criticism personally, regard it as an opportunity.

Remember that one is always selling a cure, not prevention. Prevention does not conform to the quick and easy requirement for any effective persuasion writing. Persuasion is not, in the minds of most consumers, worth spending a lot of money on. Cures, however, are oftentimes worth any amount of money, especially if they happen to be very easy and convenient cures that are relatively pain-free. Think of it in terms of maximizing pleasure and minimizing pain: Prevention tends to minimize pleasure and require painful efforts toward self-denial. Cures offer only the alleviation of a pain. It's easy to see which sales pitch requires the least amount of work on the part of the salesperson.

Don't overextend one's financial resources when launching a new product. Remember that it's very easy for even experienced and skilled investors to fall into the trap of allowing good money to follow bad. Take small steps first and test the waters. If the product shows promise, then allocate more finances toward promotion. This can include measures such as shooting video for promotion with home cameras instead of hiring a production crew and making use of a great deal of sales copy as it's one of the cheapest forms of advertising available.

If media is added to a campaign, be sure it's done right. Don't put a lot of gray space between images and text and don't allow media to interrupt the flow of text. The text must be easy to follow and not require the reader to make uncomfortable visual and mental leaps to follow what's being said.

Be honest. There is a fine line that sales copywriters tread between offering the reader a bit of shock and being realistic and honest. One does not want to end up offering up their credibility for a product that is of low quality or for cause of having made untrue claims. Being honest includes the following:

☐ Limiting special offers to a realistic time-frame

☐ Taking into account how many copies of any free demos are available

☐ Updating materials once a special offer has expired

☐ Not offering more than one can deliver

☐ Making no untrue claims regarding a product

The single most important asset a salesperson has is their credibility. Without it, they are simply a voice yelling in the wilderness that will not be heeded by any intelligent person. Remember that those customers who feel jilted will likely remember that experience for a long while and that it can take years to repair a damaged reputation.

Offer a guarantee and use your name on each letter you send out. Offer the longest-term guarantee possible. The longer the guarantee, the more a client is inclined to have faith in the product and the salesperson. Remember that vague guarantees that appeal to "satisfaction" are worthless, both to the sales effort and to the client. Never offer them. You're not cheating the client of anything worthwhile by simply skipping the entire affair.

Back up those guarantees! If a client's purchase doesn't perform as expected and they're treated respectfully and their money is refunded, they'll likely come away with a positive image of the salesperson as someone who stands behind what they offer.

Upselling a client is one of the most overlooked opportunities presented by copywriting. When that client is convinced, ready to buy and they have their credit card out, it's very easy to convince them to buy a little more.

If the customer has been persuaded into this state of mind, the copywriter has done their job. If the copywriter doesn't take advantage of their, they're not reaping the maximum possible reward for their efforts. Remember to offer a bit more and to do it in a way that lets the client know why it can be done. The importance of saying why an offer can be made cannot be overstated. People react much more positively when they're given a reason that something can be done, even if the absence of a reason would still entail a good deal for them.

Conclusion

Learning the secrets to effective copywriting is so easy and is actually so enjoyable that any businessperson who fails to do so is simply robbing themselves.

First, they're robbing themselves of the best employee they'll ever have: The humble sales letter. This letter is always on your side, always backs your product and is always possessed of the best possible sales pitch. It works tirelessly to promote your products and the techniques one develops while writing it can be used over and over again.

Second, the amount that one learns about selling their products through writing is very impressive. It may well educate the sales person about benefits their products have which they hadn't considered before. It can help one refine one's sales pitch, both in person and online and help the salesperson understand why their product is valuable.

Third, it creates an opportunity to gain more from studying the competition. The competitors for any product have certainly created their own sales copy and studying theirs can help the marketer to understand where they might fill a gap their competition hasn't yet satisfied. It can also present an opportunity to challenge the competition on several fronts. This may mean better prices, a better product or simply backing one's products with the sort of guarantees that inspire confidence and that engender customer loyalty. Standing by those guarantees is a way to turn an unsatisfied customer into one who has a great deal of confidence in one's business practices and who won't hesitate to try another product from that salesperson.

Fourth, it's a skill one can keep developing over their entire career and a skill they may well be able to sell as a separate product! Those sales copywriters who are particularly skilled come at a high price. There's no reason that an independent marketer cannot refine, develop and perfect those skills until they are among the best. Just remember that getting started means starting small and allowing one's self some room for error. Try and try again, so to speak and learn from competition where possible.

This is simply one of the most cost effective ways to advertise and really one of the most effective at reaching clients. It works on paper and online and can help one build confidence in their sales skills and realize the results of the effort invested in very short order. Where finding new ways to market a product is concerned, sometimes learning a better way to employ a very ancient skill, the written word, is among the best available.

Get Started!

Get a pen and a paper and a file folder and start collecting sales letters that do their job well. Start writing them, by hand, and understanding them.

Once you've done this, practice, practice, practice. The more you write, the better you'll get. Soon enough, you'll have developed the skills it takes to write truly effective sales copy without paying the sometimes excessive prices charged by professional copywriters. If you do it well enough, you may even be able to charge those great rates for your own copywriting services!

About the Author: Bill Price

Bill Price is a Language Coach, blogger, polyglot, and lifelong language learner. He currently resides in Denver, CO USA with his wife, Kirsten, and three children.

Website/Blog: www.howtolanguages.com

Facebook:
www.facebook.com/howtolanguages

Twitter: www.twitter.com/htlanguages

To inquire about personal language coaching, please email:
Bill@ideaseedlabs.com

Other Books by Bill Price

Calm Mind: *Discover How to Calm Your Mind, improve Your Health, and Take Control of Your Life*

Efficient Language Learning

Authority Facebook Live

Rapid Facebook Ads

Health Primal Living